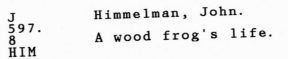
J
597.
8
HIM

Himmelman, John.

A wood frog's life.

WITHDRAWN

DATE			
	WITHDRAWN		

Nature Upclose

A Wood Frog's Life

Written and Illustrated by John Himmelman

Children's Press®
A Division of Grolier Publishing

New York London Hong Kong Sydney
Danbury, Connecticut

For my wife, Betsy, who taught me:
- *mixing a little red paint with green tones down the color*
- *not to "fight with the watercolors"*
- *to love the little froggies.*

Library of Congress Cataloging-in-Publication Data

Himmelman, John
    A wood frog's life / written and illustrated by John Himmelman.
       p.   cm. — (Nature upclose)
    Summary: Illustrations and simple text describe the daily activities and life cycle of a wood frog.
    ISBN 0-516-21178-1 (lib.bdg.)   0-516-26403-6 (pbk.)
    1. Wood frog—Juvenile literature. 2. Wood frog—Life cycles—Juvenile literature.   [1. Wood frog. 2. Frogs.] I. Title.   II. Series: Himmelman, John. Nature upclose.
QL668.E27H55   1998
597'.8'9—dc21   97-41017
                                     CIP
                                     AC

Visit Children's Press on the Internet at:
http://publishing.grolier.com

Wood Frog
Rana sylvatica

Wood frogs are common throughout eastern North America. In fact, they live as far north as the Arctic Circle!

Each spring, wood frogs gather in shallow pools of temporary water. The frogs reproduce in these pools because there are no fish to eat their eggs or tadpoles. Wood frogs spend the rest of the year in the woods because food is more plentiful. They are safest in wooded areas because their skin blends in with dead leaves. In winter, wood frogs hibernate under leaves. They have a special chemical in their blood that keeps them from freezing solid.

Every male wood frog has a voice that he uses to attract mates. When he forces air out of his lungs, it passes over vocal cords in his throat. The vocal cords vibrate and give off sound. The air also causes vocal sacs in the frog's throat and sides to puff out and make his call louder.

In spring, a wood frog lays her eggs in a pool of shallow water.

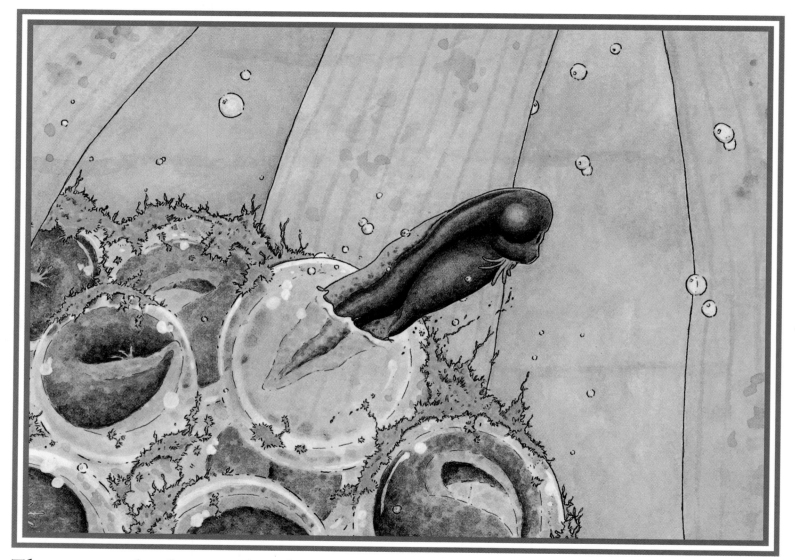

Three weeks later, the first *tadpole* hatches.

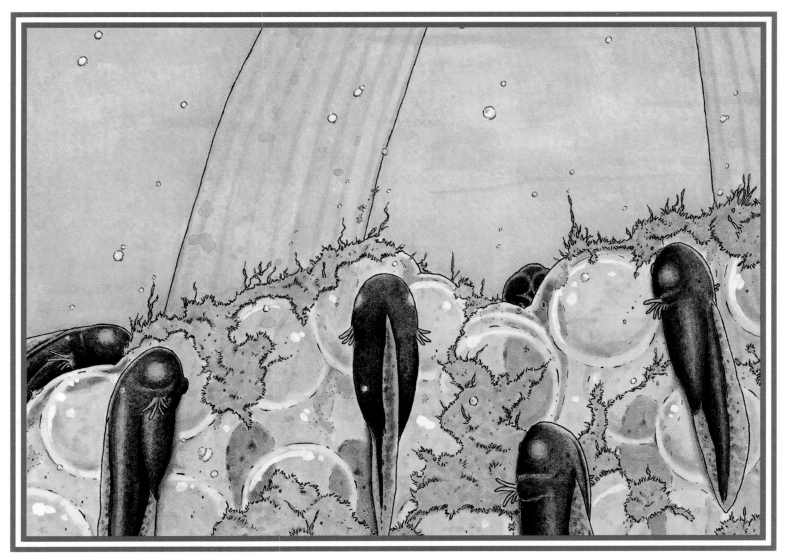

Tadpoles spend their first few days hanging from the *egg mass*.

Each tadpole munches on *algae* that grows on rocks at the bottom of the pool.

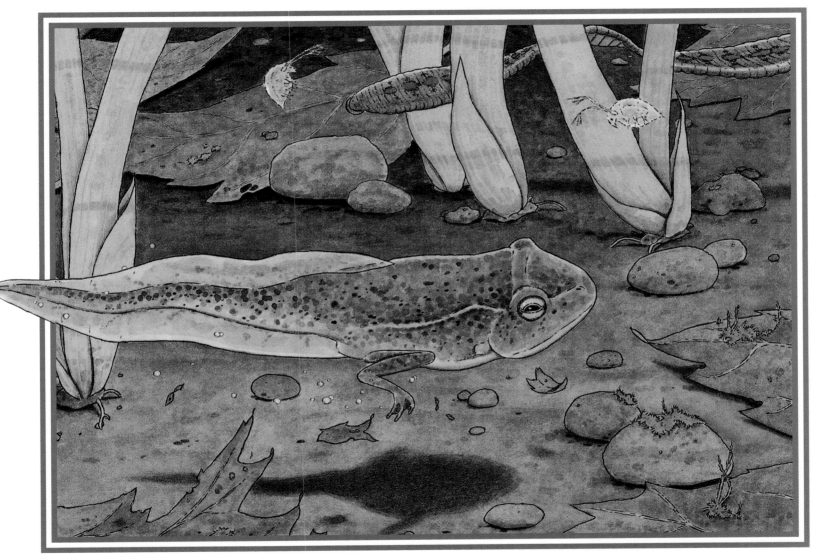

As time goes by, the tadpole grows and legs appear.

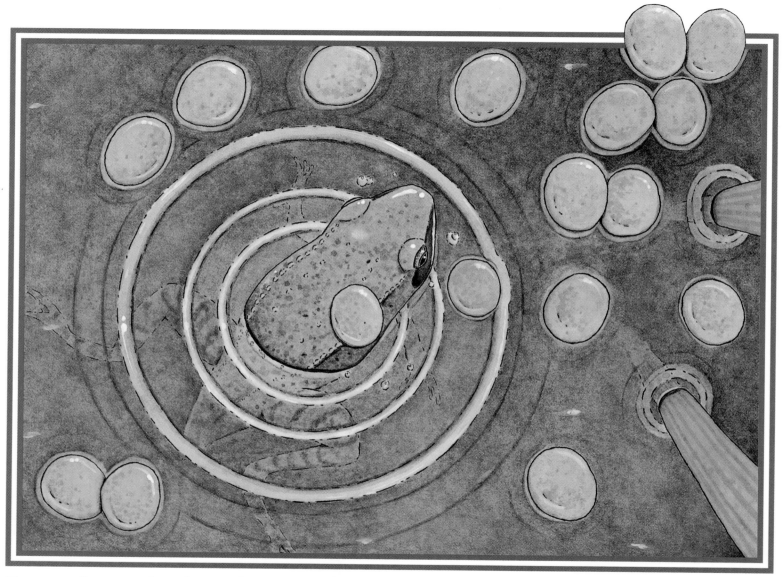

Soon the tadpole takes his first breath of air.

Just 2 months after hatching, the tadpole has turned into a frog.

He hunts for small flies near the edge of the pool.

As the frog grows, he moves farther into the woods.

The frog's skin blends with dead leaves, but some enemies can still spot him.

After a summer of eating, sleeping, hiding, and escaping, the frog gets ready for winter.

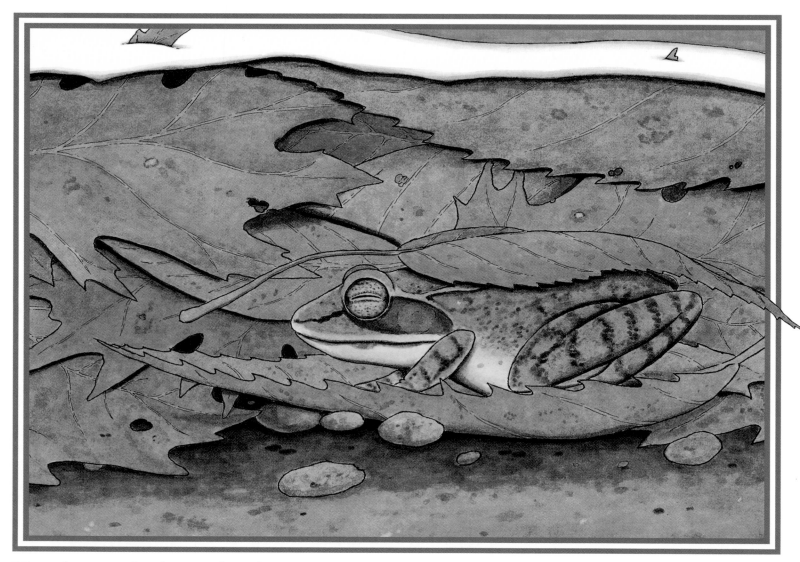

He sleeps below the leaves during the cold winter.

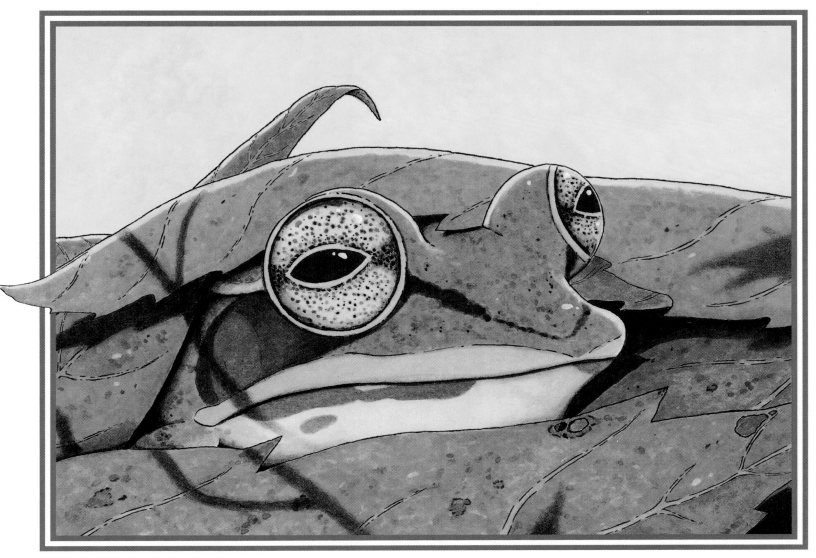

A sunny spring morning wakes the wood frog.

He looks for a shallow pool. So do other wood frogs.

For the next few days and nights, the frog is noisy. His call sounds like a quacking duck.

Then the wood frog returns to the woods. All summer he searches for food.

When the weather grows cold, he finds a cozy place to spend his second winter.

The wood frog *hibernates* through the coldest days and nights . . .

. . . and wakes up on a sunny spring afternoon.

Once again, wood frogs head toward a nearby pool of water.

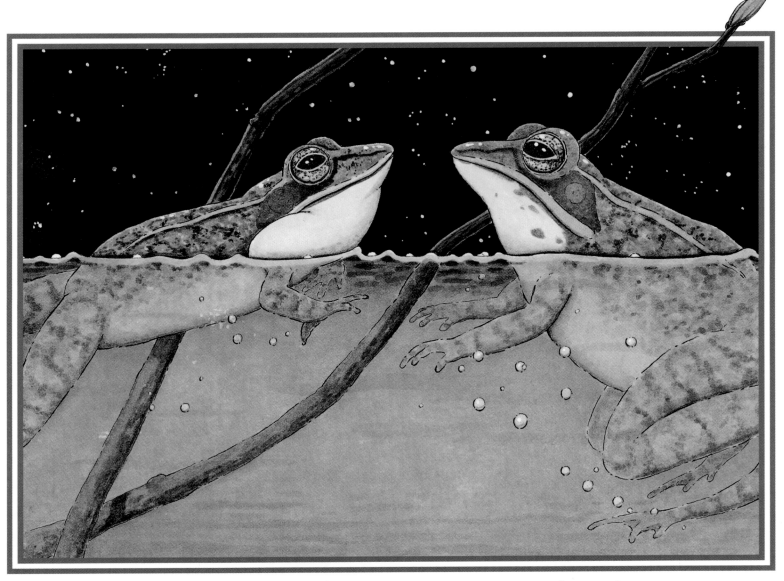

This year, the wood frog's quacking attracts a female.

The frogs mate in the water, and the female lays hundreds of eggs.

After a few days, the wood frog returns to his summer home—
the woods.

But something blocks his path.

He is kissed by a girl looking for her prince.

The girl does not harm the wood frog. She returns him to the ground.

For the rest of his years, the wood frog will spend most of his time on the forest floor.

And each spring, he will add his voice to the wood frog chorus.

Words You Know

algae—a green, slimy layer of plantlike creatures.

egg mass—a large clump of eggs and the jellylike material around them.

hibernate—to spend the winter with a slow heartbeat and breathing.

tadpole—the first stage of a frog's life.

About the Author

John Himmelman has written or illustrated more than forty books for children, including *Ibis: A True Whale Story*, *Wanted: Perfect Parents*, and *J.J. Versus the Babysitter*. His books have received honors such as Pick of the List, Book of the Month, JLG Selection, and the ABC Award. He is also a naturalist who enjoys turning over dead logs, crawling through grass, kneeling over puddles, and gazing at the sky. His greatest joy is sharing these experiences with others. John lives in Killingworth, Connecticut, with his wife Betsy who is an art teacher. They have two children, Jeff and Liz.